I CAN RUN

MARLA CONN

Rourke

Photo Glossary

 bear

 cat

 cheetah

 fox

 horse

 zebra

High Frequency Words:
- a
- can
- run

A **cat** can run.

A **horse** can run.

A **zebra** can run.

A **bear** can run.

A **cheetah** can run.

A **fox** can run.

fox

Activity

1. Name all of the animals in the story that can run.

2. Create a main idea and details chart on a separate piece of paper.

3. Discuss and chart the cause and effect relationships- Why Animals Run.
    - get away from danger (prey)
    - catch food (predator)
    - play
    - find their family
    - exercise

4. Write a sentence about one of the animals from the story. Draw a picture and share.